I'm Not Sick

Written & Illustrated By,
H. Miller

ISBN: 978-1-7344560-0-4 (Paperback)
ISBN: 978-1-7344560-1-1 (Hardcover)

Front cover image by Artist H. Miller
Book design by Designer H. Miller

Printed in USA

First printing edition 2020.

Hippocratic Oath Publishing
hippocraticoathpublishing.com

This Book Belongs to:

To my girls

for whom I would give my last breath.

To my husband

who has always been my rock and our protector.

To my family and friends whom offered encouragement.

To those that doubted me.

To all who speak up to protect our freedoms.

Truth will always prevail.

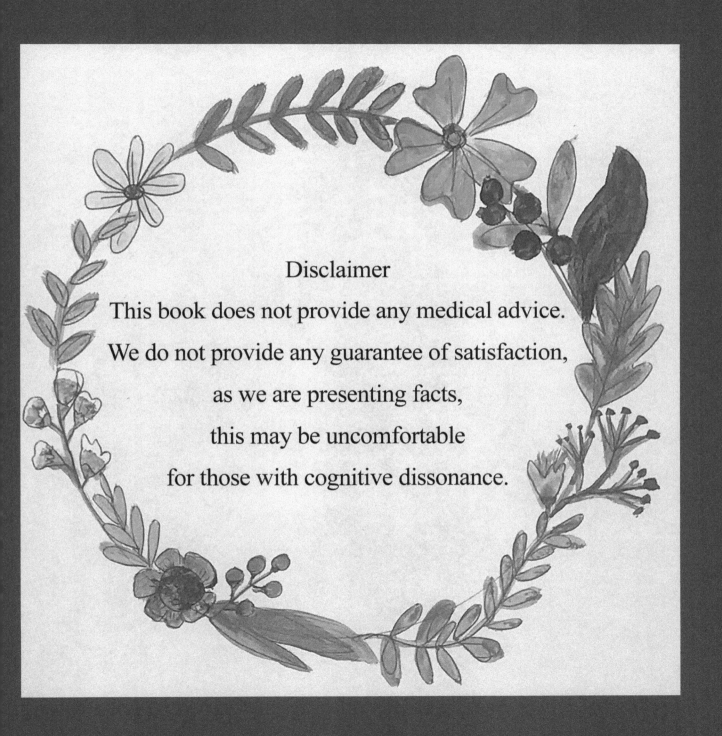

Disclaimer

This book does not provide any medical advice.

We do not provide any guarantee of satisfaction,

as we are presenting facts,

this may be uncomfortable

for those with cognitive dissonance.

Grace would like a treat.
I can't give her a candy or
something sweet because
I do not have any sweets.
I can't give her what I do not have.

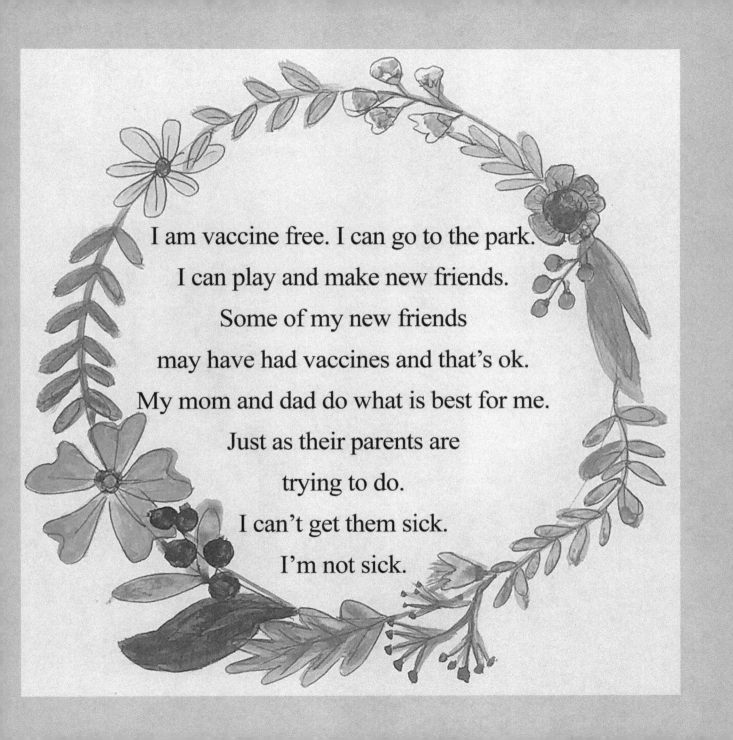

I am vaccine free. I can go to the park.

I can play and make new friends.

Some of my new friends

may have had vaccines and that's ok.

My mom and dad do what is best for me.

Just as their parents are

trying to do.

I can't get them sick.

I'm not sick.

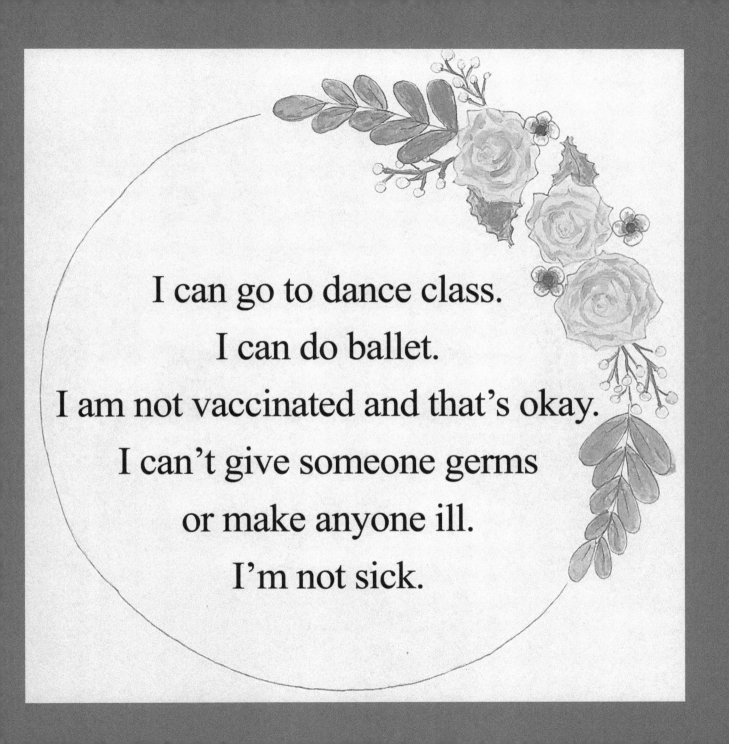

I can go to dance class.

I can do ballet.

I am not vaccinated and that's okay.

I can't give someone germs
or make anyone ill.

I'm not sick.

I can fly on a plane.

I can look at the clouds.

Most adults vaccines have long worn off.

I do not put them at risk, I am not sick.

There hasn't been herd immunity

from vaccines, that's a myth.

There aren't enough adults

vaccinated or up to date.

If we want herd immunity there is only one way,

natural immunity is the type that will stay.

But do not worry sometimes

illnesses just go away,

just look up the plague.

Clean water, and plumbing saved us

from those dark days.

I can travel the world. I am safe.

My immune system protects me.

My dad and mom had all the recommended vaccines

when they were small.

My mom got 22 shots in all,

the amount a 6 month old will have had.

That is so many. That makes me sad.

I can stay in a fancy hotel. I can stay anywhere
because I am well.
If you had some vaccines then had to stop, you can stay too.
There shouldn't be anyone worried,
because we can not give something we do not have.
If you have had all the shots or none
the only way to share germs is if you have germs to share.
Some vaccines have live viruses, so even if you don't feel ill,
you can leave germs about.
I have a healthy immune system
so that is not something I waste time worrying about.

I can go to a National Park.
Yellowstone was so fun.
I can travel.
I can meet people from all around the world.
They may like vaccines or not,
but if they are not from America, they have less shots.
I love to travel to new places.
I am not sharing germs they talk about on the news.
I hear them talk, but what they say is not true.
I am not putting anyone at risk.
I am not sick.
I am strong. I am healthy.
My immune system protects me.

I can hold a newborn baby.
A baby that is little and new.
Even if the baby's mommy is scared of illnesses
and wants to vaccinate.
I can't give the baby germs.
I have none to share because I'm not sick.

I can visit the elderly.

My great grandma has had the measles,

mumps and chicken pox.

Grandma said that the worst thing ever was when

she got the smallpox shot.

I can't put her in danger because she has natural, life-long immunity

Also, remember I can't make her sick.

I'm not sick.

I can go to a toy store.
I can play and I can shop.
You see I can go anywhere,
around anyone, because
I'm not sick.
If we have no germs to share,
we cannot make someone unwell.

I can go to school.
I have an exemption from vaccines.
Some of my friends are vaccine free,
some of my friends had vaccines,
and that's okay. We can all play.
I can't get them sick. I'm not sick.
There are lots of germs at school.
Sometimes kids go to school sick.
That's not something I do.
When I am sick I stay home.

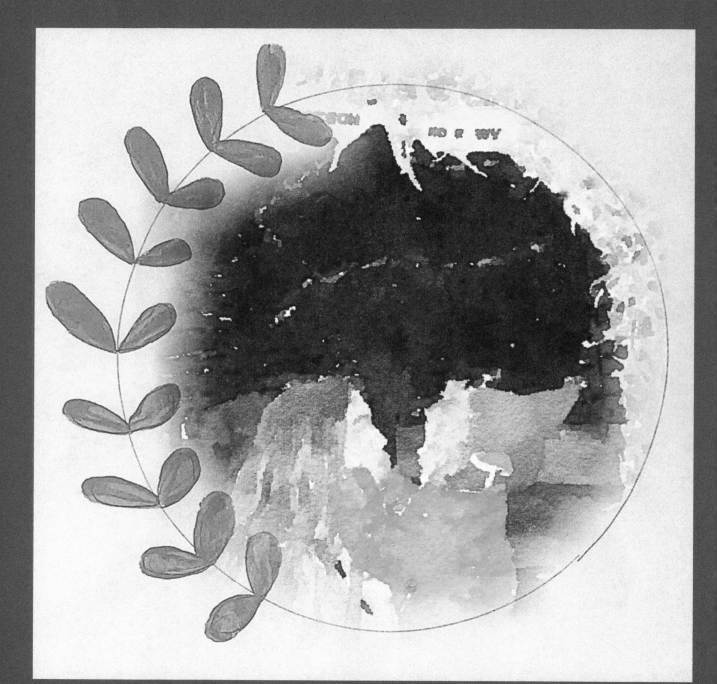

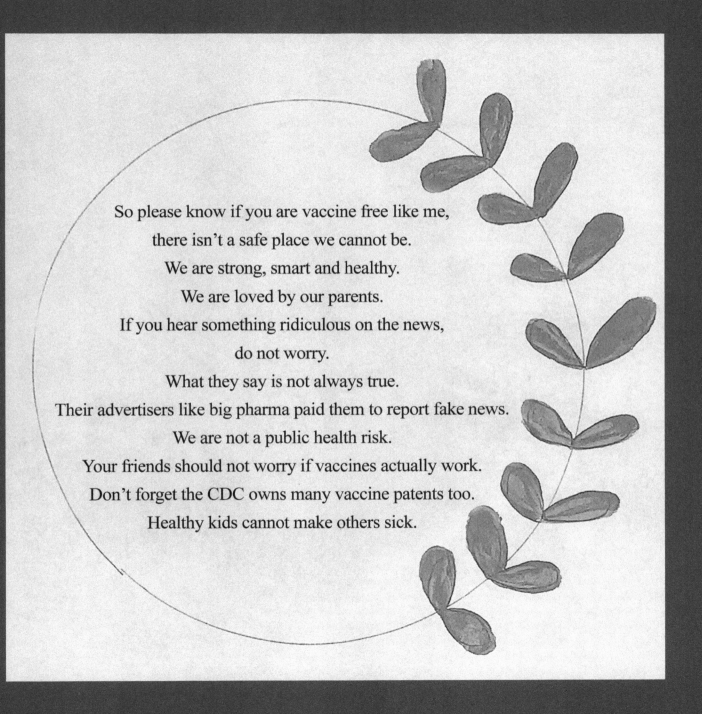

So please know if you are vaccine free like me,
there isn't a safe place we cannot be.
We are strong, smart and healthy.
We are loved by our parents.
If you hear something ridiculous on the news,
do not worry.
What they say is not always true.
Their advertisers like big pharma paid them to report fake news.
We are not a public health risk.
Your friends should not worry if vaccines actually work.
Don't forget the CDC owns many vaccine patents too.
Healthy kids cannot make others sick.

Our parents have good reasons they chose what they did.

Some of us were injured after one shot or a few.

Some lost loved ones.

Some parents trusted their guts and learned of the risks.

Some found out about the poisons and DNA contained in the shots.

Once they were informed they knew what to do.

Give your parents a hug and say thank you.

They are working so hard protecting you.

Always remember we cannot spread germs

we do not have because we are not sick.

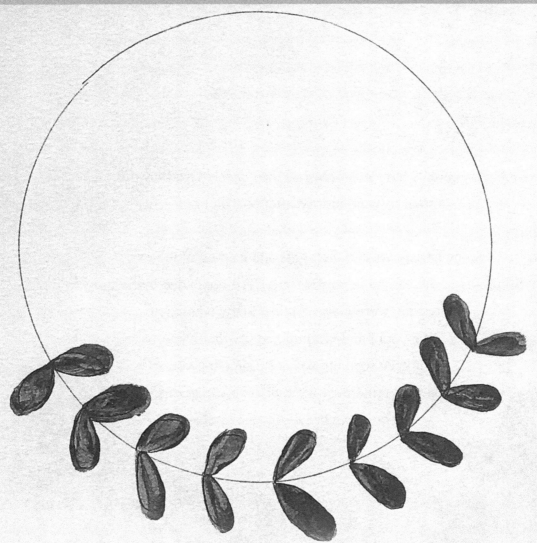

You can use these pages to share your story.
These pages are yours to list resources, scriptures and experiences
of others you may want to reference.

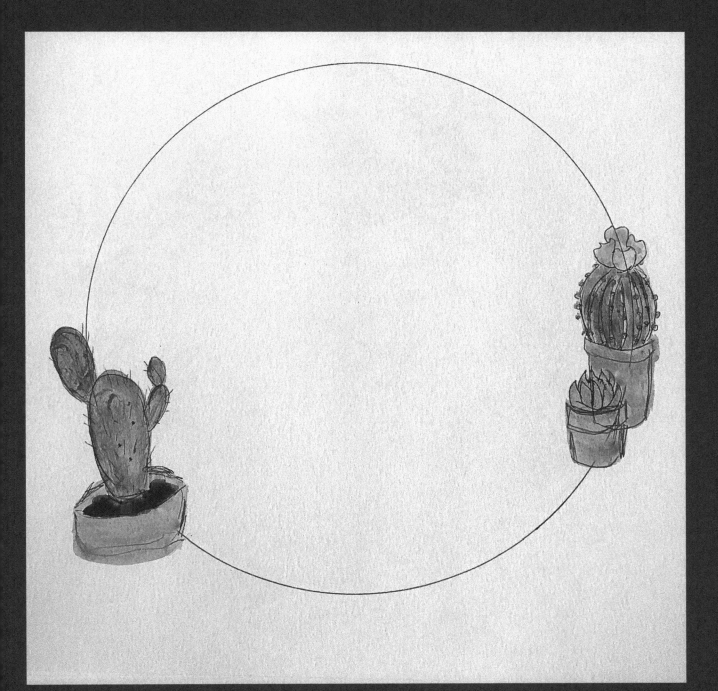

About the Author

This book is written for all caregivers who are making informed decisions for their children. This book was written so that vaccine free children do not feel isolated and discriminated against. Showing that vaccine free kids are safe, loved and healthy was the purpose of my book. It is a book that shows we can not share what we do not have.

I was once pro-vaccine, and thought anyone that wasn't going to vaccinate was crazy. I wasn't scared of unvaccinated people because I believed vaccines worked.

I had a friend that had a baby years before I did. She would call me hysterically crying before and after each "well" baby appointment. Her daughter would get fevers and sleep a lot or cry a lot. She would get rashes and lumps from the shots.

I was pro-vaccine at the time, but I told her why not stop? She said she couldn't because she had to have them for school. I knew that wasn't true because my best friend from elementary school was not vaccinated. She had a religious exemption. My friend continued to vaccinate her baby and she continued to be upset about it. It was a small seed planted for me. Her daughter developed severe eczema and digestive issues.

When I was in college, I took care of a 4-month-old when he had the measles. He was formula fed and vaccinated on schedule. He was "sick" about a week. In other words, he had a mild runny nose and a rash for about a week. He played, interacted and acted normally. He is now a healthy teenager. The measles even for the population who are not overly health conscious and with an average diet, non breastfed population is less miserable than the common cold. This was also a small seed as I saw first hand that even a small infant could easily handle the measles.

Later, when I was pregnant with our first baby we were out of town, I ended up in the hospital at 14 weeks. I had started bleeding. I was very afraid. The OB that saw me said that I would lose my baby and that I needed to be induced the next day. I was heartbroken. I asked the doctor what the chances were of losing our baby. She said she could not tell me. I asked how much of the placenta was torn, she could not tell me.

We had regular checks for our baby's heartbeat throughout the night. One nurse would not listen to us when we told her where to place the doppler on my stomach. She was in a hurry and told us there was no heartbeat. We grieved for our daughter. I was so deep in despair.

The next morning they brought in an ultra sound machine. I did not want to look. I did not want to see my sweet, once wiggly, little baby still inside my stomach. I hid my face, but my husband said, "Look, look she is still moving and her heartbeat is still just as strong."

I asked the nurse if being induced would kill my baby. She said, "Yes she would not survive." I talked with my husband. We knew that it was a risk for me to continue the pregnancy. We knew that she may not make it hours or days longer, but we both knew I could not go through with being induced which would end my pregnancy. We had to give her a chance.

My husband and I knew our baby could be developmentally delayed, but we loved her and would love her no matter what, no matter how long or short of a time we had with her. We told the OB doctor I did not want to be induced. She told us I could either be induced or leave the hospital. Do it or leave, she did not give us informed consent. She also told me I could always get pregnant again.

We made the decision to leave and we transferred to another hospital in another town. Once we met with the doctor there, she had an entirely different outlook. She said that the fluid was good, and that she was still active. The new OB doctor said that it was a waiting game to get to 24 weeks for viability out of the womb.

Once the hospital felt that I was stable they advised that we stay near by and referred us to stay at a local non-profit. After a week we felt that we needed to get home. I called my regular OB and he advised that I be seen twice weekly upon return home.

My regular OB told me that the placenta can heal as it moves up the uterus. This was a huge eye opener for me. The doctor at the hospital was not all knowing. She had never mentioned the placenta healing was a possibility, and had even told me that it wasn't when I had asked her. I had never questioned or lost trust in doctors before this. I learned the importance of second and even third opinions. I began to learn to trust my gut. I even began to regain my faith in God.

I stayed on bedrest and researched everything that nurses and doctors typically do to a newborn baby. It did not feel right to give a vaccine on day one of life. We decided to skip the hep B shot as it had risks and our daughter would not be in an environment that would expose her to risks of contracting a virus that is spread through exposure to bodily fluids of an infected person.

I talked with my OB about the Vitamin K shot. I was told it was just a vitamin. Sadly I did not do further research. I trusted my doctor.

My daughter was born via emergency c-section after a failed attempt to induce me, due to growth restrictions, and not passing a non-stress test. She was born with a high APGAR score weighing 4 pounds 7 ounces, and 17 inches long. She was so tiny but she was very alert. We declined the hep B shot but she got the Vitamin K shot.

Our newborn, preemie, daughter went from attempting to nurse, taking a bottle and smiling at her momma to lethargic, with severe stress on her liver needing to be in the incubator, having her stomach pumped multiple times, needing a feeding tube.

We nearly lost her. She could not tolerate the neurological toxin overload that is the Vitamin K shot. An injection with a black box warning, that I was not shown. I did not have informed consent even when I had asked questions about it. This was another seed planted.

We continued to research and it took us at least two years of solid research to go from delaying vaccines until after she was two to knowing that we could never risk her life, to finding out that the vaccines contained human fetal DNA and animal DNA and were against our religious beliefs. This was all before I ever joined a Facebook group. My husband and I did scholarly searches and read every study we could find. We compared the adverse reactions to vaccines listed on the CDC and vaccine inserts to the risks of contracting the illnesses. We compared the US schedule to world wide schedules. We made the informed decision to not vaccinate.

At first my dad was not supportive. I am known for having the last word. I made him read studies, I read them to him, and I talked about it with him for months. Eventually, he agreed that I was right, but he told me it was difficult to hear about how bad vaccines are when he vaccinated my brother and I. It was difficult to admit that he made the wrong decision for us. It was difficult to understand how the government could keep recommending them knowing the risks. My brother, a college student at the time, read what I sent him, and decided to change his degree being frustrated with the bias of his pre-med classes.

We faced some backlash when I first posted on Facebook questioning vaccine safety. It was hard at first but eventually people came around to understanding or respecting our decision. I kept sharing and I had people coming to me to ask about exemptions. I shared information and put a lot of energy into reaching out to pregnant friends and family members warning them of risks associated with vaccines.

My daughter, about four years old at the time, was exposed to the measles at dance class, by a vaccinated little girl. The girl was sneezing and coughing all over. I thought to myself, "Why the heck don't people keep their sick kids at home?" We got a call the next day from one of the dance moms that the little girl had the measles. NO, it didn't make the news, SHOCKING. I gave my daughter some vitamin C and A and she never got the measles. My daughter was mostly formula fed and a preemie and completely unvaccinated. Some would say that she would have been at a greater risk for catching something like the measles.

She was also accidentally exposed to whooping cough (Pertussis) by her babysitter who swore she just had allergies. Once again, we did not get sick. The babysitter was fully vaccinated and so were her two little sisters who also got pertussis. There is a study that shows the DTaP actually negatively impacts immunity life long. https://www.ncbi.nlm.nih.gov/m/pubmed/30793754/

Where there is risk there must be choice. We cannot continue to blame the vaccine free population for outbreaks when anyone that has received a live virus vaccine can shed the illness. We cannot continue to repeat the mantra that vaccines are "safe and effective" while they have been ruled "unavoidably unsafe" by the US Supreme Court.

Federally mandated vaccination is a violation of our constitutional rights. I have two perfectly healthy unvaccinated little girls. They go to the doctor so rarely that the office usually tries to charge us a new patient fee each time.

Years back when I was having the placental abruption at the hospital, blood tests for genetic reasoning for the pregnancy complications revealed I had a clotting disorder. This disorder actually makes it harder for my body to detox vaccine adjuvants and other toxins. We decided to have genetic testing done on our girls, and they also have the condition. This means we have increased risk factors for adverse reactions from vaccines. Besides the medical risks, the inefficient evidence of safety, the increased susceptibility to illness and other risks involved, we are also religiously against vaccination due to the use of human fetal DNA and Animal DNA. See the CDC chart listing vaccinate with excipients or go to FDA.gov to find vaccine inserts.

We should not let this issue divide families and friends. I hope that this book can explain why vaccine choice is not only safe for your kids but everyone. Medical decisions are not anyone else's business and should be decided by parents and patients, rather than government and doctors that both profit from the procedure.

We are facing pressure worldwide to choose between medical freedom or perceived security. I assure you, we are safer with freedoms than we are without them. Please do not let fear drive you. I hope you can all find courage and strength to continue to share the importance of informed consent and medical freedom.

CPSIA information can be obtained
at www.ICGtesting.com
Printed in the USA
JSHW011932250720
6796JS00002B/33